Government Customer Service Standards

Daryl Covey

C_{gov}

Community of Practice

May, 2012

DEDICATION

This book is dedicated to my colleagues who answered the call and came together to create something we all believed in so strongly that we worked by consensus. Your collective vast knowledge of contact services in the public sector has given this work the intrinsic viability, credibility, and usability befitting an open standard for government services. I thank you on behalf of citizens everywhere for making time beyond your regular duties to make a difference in government.

"Great events are but the sum total of the personalities behind them."

– Francis Trevelyan Miller

Daryl Covey
May, 2012

ACKNOWLEDGEMENTS

The vision and leadership of Mr. James Vaughn led to the launch of our interagency Committee. Mr. Stuart Willoughby was our guiding mentor. Ms. Karen Trebon kept the Committee's approach to the work systematic. As we completed our work, Mr. Robert Smudde – new to government at the time but expert in private sector service practices — became our tireless advocate and champion. A variety of reviewing organizations added perspective and applicability from their collective public sector expertise. I am truly grateful to my agency management for allowing me to devote most of my time to the Committee's work as a capstone leadership development assignment.

CONTENTS

PREFACE

We are all customers of government in many ways. We each deal with government throughout the course of our lives, adapting as we do so to the various service paradigms for paying taxes, reporting crimes, buying bonds and car tags, summoning emergency help, paying postage, applying for retirement benefits, and much more. From the teenager getting their first driver's license to the owner of a small business with a long-term government loan, we all interact with government as an integral part of our daily lives.

As we each navigate our own *government universe* -- comprised of the government offices we individually deal with and the specific ways we interact with each of them -- the only consistency we typically encounter is *inconsistency*! Every entity of government employs their own unique mix of contact channels, service levels, information capture, privacy policies, knowledge management, and customer focus to deliver services. There is no shared common baseline! In order for government to finally step out as a player in the 21st Century service arena, we must first master our greatest challenge:

Customers of government today must involuntarily adapt as they move between organizations to an endless array of service paradigms

It's time to conquer this barrier to excellence and move our services to a higher plane of responsiveness and consistency for the benefit of our collective customers – the entire human race!

INTRODUCTION

In March of 2005 I received a telephone call in Juneau, Alaska, where I was completing a temporary assignment as part of my agency's leadership development program. I had just finished the first of three such assignments during the prior fall in Washington, DC and had not yet identified the final one. As the conversation progressed, I became increasingly enthralled with both the idea presented and the related challenge. Near the end of the discussion, I was asked if I would chair a working group developing citizen contact service guidance for the United States Government. I readily agreed, and by mid-May I was heading home to reunite with my family and begin this new labor of love as my crowning assignment.

During the late spring of that year, as I was wrapping up my work in Alaska, the U. S. General Services Administration reached out across the federal government to solicit volunteer customer contact service managers for our interagency Committee. This group ultimately grew to fifty eight participants from thirty three departments and agencies as well as the Smithsonian Institution (a trust). The members represented an amazing array of constituencies, lines of business[1], contact volumes, and service paradigms. Given the breadth of our participation and the goal of our work, this was shaping up to be a truly landmark step for government services. But given the deadline of October first to complete our task, we were facing a long summer of serious work. For most of us, this work would have to be accomplished in addition to our "real job" without adverse impact to the latter!

In early July we agreed on initial guiding principles for our work and decided to form five working groups to draft guidance for review by the full Committee. Four of the working groups were devoted, respectively, to: (1) telephone; (2) email; (3) "traditional" channels (walk-in, postal mail, and facsimile); and (4) "future" methods (video, instant messaging, chat, etc.). The fifth group was tasked to develop guidance applicable across all customer contact channels based on the work of the other groups. Individual Committee members were free to work wherever they thought their experience and interests would best contribute to the results. Some busy individuals could only participate in one working group, while most chose more than one. A few (including me) participated in all five. The groups began their work with weekly teleconferences and open exchange of ideas between those meetings. The project was rolling and interest was very high!

By late August, drafts from the various working groups were in review by the full Committee. Later a complete draft was reviewed externally by representatives of state and local governments, foreign governments, nonprofits, academia, and other key interest groups. Finally, in early October, our complete results were presented to a special meeting of federal agency representatives, and soon afterward were mailed to the head of every federal department and agency. We received many accolades for our work and celebrated our success. We were proud, excited, and anticipating the future impacts of what we'd done. Then the music died and the stage went dark. *What happened?*

Living in the country gives me a tremendous opportunity to observe the night sky, far from city lights. Many evenings I linger outside after my chores are done to watch the moon, stars, and planets appear as the twilight fades. It's a magnificent, ever-changing picture which is amazingly predictable by astronomers. When a big event (comet, meteor shower, planet alignment, etc.) occurs, you have to view it at precisely the right time -- then it's gone! Likewise, for great events to happen in government, it's often said that the "stars must align" -- but it's not always so predictable. It takes the right time, politics, talent, leadership, and priority from the top. And then, as soon as it finally happens, something else immediately supplants it as the new cause *du jour!* Our sector doesn't typically spend a lot of time and energy reflecting on what's already been done, perhaps because there's always so much more still left to do. As my friend Yolunda Davis wisely says, *"We're always looking for the next big shiny thing!"*

The work of our Committee members with many hundreds of years of collective experience as both government contact service managers and citizen customers to create an open standard for serving citizens is unprecedented. But by the time it was completed, a new fiscal year had begun, the movers and shakers had new annual performance goals, and a national election was rising on the distant horizon. The fleeting spotlight of government quickly shifted to the next stellar attraction.

Today, the stars are again shining -- this time even more brightly -- on the quality of government's services to citizens. It's a prime time to reintroduce the results of this landmark effort. The body of knowledge which we painstakingly assimilated and unanimously endorsed is now reintroduced as a resource to help move government services everywhere to new levels of effectiveness. In the words of the Committee,

"The enticement to resource and utilize our endorsed practices and approaches will, we hope, lie ultimately in the impressiveness of the results from doing so."

* * *

[1] Lines of business for government contact services are shown in Appendix 3.

GUIDING PRINCIPLES

The respondents to the call for Committee volunteers, and the organizations they represented, were a collage of customer contact service diversity.[1] Some of them were focused primarily upon only one channel, others on multichannel support. Many were most interested in the more "traditional" contact channels, while many more were exploring, or at least anticipating, the vast service potential of the world-wide-web. A vocal few were very concerned about creating new unfunded requirements without providing the additional budget to meet them. Perhaps a few even joined in part to enhance their political visibility (just a hunch). But to a person they each brought a strong desire to improve government's contact services by applying their experience as both citizens and service managers. We unified early around this shared goal to collaborate and create for the greater good throughout the course of our work.

As the facilitator for all five working groups and co-chair for the full Committee, I was continually impressed with the professionalism displayed by our members — even when dealing with the most relatively divisive topics. It made such a massive and complex undertaking possible, enjoyable, and eventually highly successful. When disagreements

arose, as they were certain to do given our complex mix of
perspectives, each person who wished to be was politely
heard. Then we worked collegially as a group until agreement
was reached. Below are the six guiding principles which we
adopted and refined along the way to facilitate our work.

1. Customer View

As our working groups launched on their respective tasks,
the overarching charge at the outset was to *put ourselves in
the shoes of our customers and envision what is "right" in serving
them.* For our diverse group of contact service managers,
each accustomed to struggling daily to balance service
effectiveness with service efficiency, this was a refreshing
new approach. For some, it was their first real opportunity to
ponder fully without distraction what "right" looks like for
the citizen customer, and they adapted well!

2. Resource Allocation

Despite working primarily from the customer view, we
could not completely detach ourselves from our fiduciary
responsibility to utilize resources carefully in serving the
customers who are required to provide them in the form of
taxes. This was a particular concern for those representing
organizations with high contact volumes in traditional

channels. It was ultimately addressed with a special appendix[2] and also at the beginning of our report as follows:

"The capacity of agencies to fully adopt the practices and approaches endorsed by the Committee is a function of size and resources."

Incorporation of this caveat liberated hesitant members to more thoughtfully consider what's really "right" in serving citizens.

3. Deference to Statutes

From the outset the Committee acknowledged that government organizations are subject to a wide and continually evolving variety of statutory requirements based on their respective line(s) of business, constituencies, services provided, contact channels utilized, privacy considerations, business cycle seasonality, and other factors. It was accordingly noted in our final report that the guidance generated by the Committee was *in no way intended to supersede any governing statutes.*

4. Levels of Endorsement

Given the huge variance in the immediacy of customer needs and impact for various services across government, not all of the guidance we developed could be endorsed at the same level of priority across all organizations. There also needed to be some inherent latitude for organizations to adapt over time toward the full service paradigm we were proposing. We accordingly developed our own tiered system of endorsement defined as follows, in *descending order of emphasis*:

Standard: "*S*"   All organizations should adhere[3]

Guideline: "*G*"   Demonstrated positive impact on customer satisfaction

Recommendation: "*R*"   Suggested improvement at organizational discretion

This framework came to be referenced in the course of our work as "*SGR*," and it was often pivotal to our ability to concur as a group. Not everything we each knew was "right" could be considered equally essential across all organizations. The real horse-trading in working group deliberations was very often related to the level of endorsement to be assigned to a specific provision.

Note: The level of endorsement assigned by the Committee to each service provision is shown in Appendix 4.

5. *Think and Revisit*

Our Committee members were each very passionate about government services and the methods used to deliver them. When differences of opinion arose during the course of our work, we would usually listen, think, create, and then compromise to move forward. But occasionally we needed time to reflect individually away from the discussions before making a final decision as a group. In those situations, we would capture the controversial issue to be reconsidered at the start of the next meeting, and then move on. This approach always worked in terms of producing a final unanimous group decision.

6. *Consensus*

The guiding principles above made it possible for us to work by consensus, which we chose at the outset of our work to do. Sometimes this approach made progress relatively slow – but the time investment was always well-returned in group synergy and, ultimately, in the quality of the results.

* * *

[1] Federal departments and agencies represented on the Committee are listed in Appendix 1.

[2] The appendix on resourcing considerations from the original report is shared in part here as Appendix 2.

[3] The term "standard" does not signify a mandate, but rather the Committee's highest level of endorsement.

All Contact Services

When citizens seek assistance, their universal goal is a *quick, accurate, courteous solution* to their issue. In the course of identifying practices to deliver this via various contact channels, the Committee identified overarching guidance applicable to *any situation where a customer touches Government.* It is the heart of our work!

Measures

1. Customer satisfaction should be measured at least annually.

2. The quality of customer service should be evaluated across all customer contact channels at least quarterly.

Service Quality

1. Resolution of customer issues during the first contact should be recognized as a key performance indicator.

2. The customer relationship management philosophy of creative and proactive customer service should be applied within the unique fiduciary and privacy constraints of government.[1]

3. Records of prior contacts should be used to minimize the need for repetition by customers.

4. Customers should have the option to communicate with a supervisor upon request.

5. Customer service representatives should use plain language.[2]

6. The use of technical terms and acronyms in customer communications should be as limited as possible.

7. Acronyms should be defined whenever used in customer communications.

8. Customers should be told when their interactions are monitored or recorded.

9. Customers should be told when information on their inquiry is being retained for future reference.

10. Frequent customers should not be asked excessively to respond to event-based surveys.

11. Lessons learned from customer feedback should be incorporated into training and service improvement in a timely manner.

12. Organizations should continuously reassess their hours of operation relative to customer needs and preferences.

13. Priority should be given to making service quality improvements in customer contact channels where quality has been indicated to be significantly lower than for other channels.[3]

Customer Complaints

1. Customers should have the option to complain via the contact channel of their choice.

2. Complaints should be acknowledged and processed in a specified and timely manner.

3. Customers submitting complaints should have the choice of whether a response is to be provided to them.

4. Customers requesting a response to their complaint should receive it in a timely manner.

5. Complaints should be evaluated to identify service improvement opportunities.

6. Complaints should be processed in a manner which assures a full, holistic view of all complaints received across all contact channels.

7. Complaints should be evaluated separately for each channel, with priority given to those channels which are the subject of relatively more complaints.

8. Lessons learned from the processing of complaints should be incorporated into training and service improvement.

Internal Processes

1. Organizations handling large volumes of customer contacts should consider using case numbers for tracking.

2. The volume and complexity of customer inquiries should be tracked and used to forecast workload and schedule customer service staffing commensurately.

3. Organizations should ensure that other entities which may refer customer contacts to them always have correct contact information.

4. The methods used to evaluate service quality should facilitate comparison between channels for improvement purposes.

5. The methods used to evaluate service quality should facilitate comparison between customer service representatives for improvement purposes.

Resource Allocation

1. Application of resources across customer contact channels should be optimized based upon the organization's size, mission, and customer feedback.

2. Continuously-available and relatively cost-efficient channels should be creatively promoted to customers utilizing other contact channels.

3. Creative forms of work scheduling should be applied to help meet customer needs and preferences for expanded hours of customer service.

Written Communications

1. Each organization should use a style guide to ensure consistency in written customer communications.

2. Style guides should address all types of written customer communications in use by the organization.

3. Style guides should promote use of plain language.

4. Style guides should specify standard greeting(s), closing(s), and signature format(s).

5. Style guides should be regularly reviewed and updated as needed.

6. Prepared scripts for communicating with customers in any channel should use plain language.

7. Customer service representatives who interact with customers in writing should be evaluated on their adherence to the style guide.

Language Services

1. The quality of language translations should take precedence over the number of languages offered.

2. Automated language translations should be validated as often as needed to ensure accuracy and customer usability.

3. Each organization should monitor and respond to the evolving needs of their constituency for language capabilities.

* * *

[1] A concept also known as Citizen Relationship Management [abbreviated "CzRM"]

[2] Plain language is communication at a level of complexity which is readily understandable by a majority of the constituency.

[3] Based on results of quality assurance activities and/or customer surveys

Telephone Services

"Understand that every time you answer the phone, you are the whole organization to that customer."

– Wendi Pomerance Brick

We have all experienced the pain as telephone customers of poorly-designed automated answering systems, periods of silence while awaiting service, and having our call disconnected during the transfer process. Yet the telephone channel continues to be the leading method of contacting government, even as new and more glamorous channels emerge. The advent of widespread mobile telephone use has only enhanced this standing.

The following provisions apply to the telephone contact channel in addition to the provisions of Section One.

Measures

1. At least eighty percent of incoming calls should be answered within sixty seconds.[1]

2. Callers who will be waiting for more than thirty seconds to speak to a customer service representative should be informed of the expected duration of their wait.

3. Call abandonment rates should not exceed four percent.[2]

4. Return calls in response to customer voice mail messages should be made no later than the next business day.

5. Up to three attempts should be made to return calls to a customer.[3]

Telephone Accessibility

1. Telephone numbers for the organization should be listed in the government sections of telephone directories.

2. Telephone numbers for the organization should be easily located on-line.

3. Toll-free calling should be provided within the organization's geographic area of jurisdiction.

Call Transfers

Before a call is transferred, the customer should be advised regarding:

(1) where their call is being transferred

(2) why their call is being transferred there

(3) a telephone number to reconnect[4] if disconnected in the process

Recorded Messages

1. FAQs or music should be played to callers in queue.[5]

2. Other continuously-available channels and relatively cost-efficient channels should be creatively promoted to telephone customers in queue.

3. Recorded information provided to callers after-hours should include hours of operation and encourage callers to use alternative service options available in the interim.

4. The same voice and personality should be used in all recordings for customers.[6]

Interactive Voice Response Systems[7]

1. Voice recognition, keypad response, and options for direct routing to a customer service representative should all be considered for inclusion.[8]

2. Customer-facing functionality[9] should be carefully determined by considering customer preferences and the complexity and volume of calls.

3. Voice prompts should provide the number to say (or press) *after* the description of the function which doing so will initiate.

4. New and infrequent users should be offered guidance on how to use the systems they are accessing.

Voice Over Internet Protocol[10]

1. Sound quality should be validated in advance of use.

2. Backup communications for use in the event of internet connectivity outages should be considered.

* * *

[1] Measured on a monthly basis

[2] Measured on an annual basis

[3] Using the information provided by the customer

[4] If possible

[5] *"FAQ"* in this section refers to voice recordings of prepared solutions to the most frequently-received inquiries from customers. It is the recommended option here due to the inherent self-service opportunity for customers while awaiting service. The alternative, music, confirms a continuing connection to customers in the telephone queue.

[6] An exception was noted for responses to unpredicted "spikes" in incoming call volume

[7] Abbreviated "IVRS" and refers to automation for processing customer contacts in the telephone channel which offers callers service and/or information options among which they can select

[8] The primary intent was to accommodate customers with disabilities as fully as possible

[9] This includes number of options per level, number of levels offered, and at what stage of system navigation the "live help" option is first offered

[10] Abbreviated "VOIP" and refers to transmission of speech across the Internet

Email and Web Response Form Services

Email accounts for a substantial share of citizen contacts with government – typically second only to the telephone channel in volume. Our sector's greatest shared challenges for this channel are acknowledging receipt of email *and* providing a timely reply every time. Similar challenges apply to services provided via the web response form[1] channel.

The following provisions apply to the email and web response form contact channels in addition to the provisions of Section One which include provisions for *all* written customer communications.

Measures

1. Response time for customer email should be determined as follows:

   a. *Relatively simple and/or common questions* should be answered at least ninety percent of the time within two business days.[2]

   b. *More complex questions involving research, management sign-off, multiple topics, and/or multiple organizations* should be answered at least ninety percent of the time within five business days.[3]

   c. *Questions which involve personal data, complex policy, scientific issues, and/or time-consuming research* should be initially responded to by email within two business days citing the complexity of the inquiry and providing an estimate of when the customer will receive a complete answer.[4]

2. When a response to customer email is unsuccessful due to spam filters or other factors beyond organizational control, two additional response attempts should be made.

Email

1. Unless they will be responded to no later than the next business day, *all* customer emails should be acknowledged

upon receipt with an automated email acknowledgement which:

   (1) reminds the sender to ensure that a response from the agency's email address can pass through any spam filters they have in place.

   (2) suggests any other available contact channels where the customer might get a faster response if it is needed.

2. Email addresses designated for customer contacts should be monitored continuously during scheduled hours of email channel availability.

3. Organizations using identifying numbers for tracking customer inquiries should always reference them in related emails.

4. Email responses should be as concise as possible given the nature of the inquiry.

5. All email responses should include links to the organization's privacy policy.

6. The sender of a misdirected email from outside the organization which is being forwarded elsewhere should be advised regarding:

   (1) where it is being forwarded

   (2) why it is being forwarded there

(3) how they can follow up if no reply is received within a reasonable time.

7. Documented procedures should be in place for handling misdirected *internal* email.

8. Organizations should monitor the evolution of methods to verify email sender identification and incorporate them at the appropriate level of maturity.[5]

9. Customer use of individual employee email addresses should be minimized.

10. Organizational use of email addresses from non-government web domains is *strongly* discouraged.

Web Response Forms

1. Web response forms should begin with a link to *FAQs*.

2. Mandatory fields should be limited to the minimum required to respond.

3. Drop-down menus should be used to allow customers to categorize the topics of their inquiries.

4. The customer should be able to choose how they wish to be responded to.[6]

5. Customers should be reminded to ensure that a response from the agency's email address can pass through their spam filters.[7]

6. Links to the organizational privacy policy should be displayed with web response forms.

7. The date and time of response to inquiries should be automatically captured.[8]

8. Use of this channel is strongly *encouraged* as an alternative to incoming customer email *if needed* to minimize the adverse impacts of spam on agency resources.

* * *

[1] "Web Response Form" here refers to the entry point for structured text information provided by customers interacting from the organization's web page for later response.

[2] Alternative channels should be suggested where the customer might find the answer sooner.

[3] The customer should be advised within two business days of the status and estimated response time.

[4] Every five to ten business days afterward, an email should update the customer as much as possible, until a complete response is provided.

[5] This applies especially to organizations whose mission requires customers to provide personal information and/or data in email transactions

[6] Customer's choice among the contact channels in use by the organization

[7] Applies if the response is to be made via email

[8] To facilitate tracking and monitoring of response times

Mail and Facsimile Services

Although it is often perceived as a somewhat archaic contact channel in the private sector, many government organizations continue to receive large volumes of citizen contacts by mail. This form of interaction is still strongly preferred by some constituencies and for some types of customer issues. The facsimile channel is addressed here as the relatively newer means for interaction with government via letter.

The following provisions apply to the mail and facsimile contact channels in addition to the provisions of Section One which include provisions for all written customer communications.

Measures

1. Customer mail should be acknowledged by mail with an estimated response time if a complete answer cannot be provided to the customer within fifteen working days.

2. Inquiries received via facsimile should be responded to by either mail or facsimile within fifteen working days.

Other Provisions

1. The topic, date of receipt, and date of response should be tracked for all mail and facsimile inquiries.[1]

2. Internal routing and processing procedures should be in place for:
    (1) letters[2] addressed to the leadership of the agency.
    (2) letters for which the intended recipient is not clear.

3. Use of facsimile in lieu of mail should be considered *as needed* when special mail screening security procedures are in place.

* * *

[1] The intended purpose is to ensure that all mail and facsimile inquiries are responded to.

[2] Both mail and facsimile

Walk-In Services

Visiting a government office to interact person-to-person continues to be strongly preferred by some constituencies, and is still *required* for certain types of transactions at all levels of government. Some of the most negative stereotypes of government service are related to this access channel.[1] These hopefully can be dispelled through implementation of the practices below.

The following provisions apply to walk-in customers in addition to the provisions of Section One.

Measures

1. Walk-in customers should be waited on in fifteen minutes or less.

2. Use of appointments should be considered when transactions typically require more than fifteen minutes.

Other Provisions

1. Walk-in customers should be given the opportunity to speak to a reception person upon arrival.

2. Organizations should ensure that walk-in customers without appointments are served in the order of their arrival.[2]

3. When walk-in customer volume warrants, a greeter should provide each arriving customer an estimate of wait time and verify that they have everything with them which is required to conduct their intended transaction.

4. When appointments are used, staffing should be scheduled accordingly to minimize customer waiting time.

5. Waiting customers *with* appointments should be able to sit or otherwise relax instead of standing in line.

6. Organizations should continually evaluate their hours of operation with respect to the evolving needs and convenience of their walk-in customers and use creative work scheduling to help respond.

7. Extended hours of operation should be considered for the convenience of walk-in customers who cannot visit during normal business hours.

8. Continuously-available channels and relatively cost-efficient channels should be creatively promoted in walk-in customer waiting areas.

* * *

[1] Long lines of people found preserved in the ashes of ancient Pompeii are rumored to have been awaiting service in government offices.

[2] Using manual "take-a-number" systems, electronic self-registration, or other methods

Web Services

"If you want to increase call volume into your call center, add more self-service options."

—Gary Lemke

The power of the world-wide-web as a channel for serving government's customers is tremendous, but *not* free or automatically-realized. Only careful customer-centric design and continuous refinement will make and keep web-based services responsive to evolving citizen needs and preferences. Web self-service in particular requires ongoing careful attention to customer needs and habits in order to remain a viable service alternative.

The following provisions apply to the web contact channel in addition to the provisions of Section One.

Measures

1. The prepared content of automated responses to customer inquiries should be reviewed and updated as needed at least quarterly.

2. *FAQs*[1] should be reviewed and updated as needed at least annually.

Posted Contact Information

1. The organization's home page should contain a prominent link to the "contact us" page.

2. "Contact us" web pages should provide information needed to reach the organization via all available customer contact channels.

3. Organizational email addresses and links to web response forms should be prominent on websites.

4. Contact information for other government organizations posted on-line should be coordinated with them in advance of posting.[2]

FAQs

1. *FAQs* should be prominently accessible from the organization's home page.

2. The *FAQs* used most often by customers should be displayed most prominently.

3. Further inquiry by customers whose issues could not be fully resolved using *FAQs* should be facilitated in a manner convenient to the customer.[3]

4. The organizational entity responsible for *FAQs* should be documented and easily contacted from *within* the organization.

5. The effectiveness of individual *FAQs* in resolving customer issues should be monitored through customer feedback.

6. Customer recommendations for changes to *FAQs* should be acknowledged and acted upon, if appropriate, in a timely manner.

7. *FAQs* available to customers should also be made available to all customer service representatives.

8. Organizations should monitor how often individual *FAQs* are used by customers.

9. Organizations should monitor the impacts of updates to *FAQs* on customer contact volume in other channels.

Really Simple Syndication[4]

1. Notifications to customers should include content descriptions in addition to titles.

2. No particular reader(s) should be recommended.

3. Customers should be offered a list of examples and/or advised to use web search to obtain readers.

4. Organizations should periodically test their web site content with various readers to ensure broad compatibility.

Web Chat

1. Hours of chat availability should be publicized if less than continuous.

2. Alternatives for service should be suggested for use by customers during any times when web chat is not available.

3. The maximum number of simultaneous chat sessions permitted to be handled by each customer service representative should not compromise service quality.

4. Customers should be offered a transcript at the end of their chat session.

Web Site Utility

1. User convenience[5] should be incorporated into web site design.

2. Organizations should study how customers search[6] on their web sites in order to enhance search effectiveness.

3. The personality of automated web responses should be chosen to maximize effectiveness in serving the organization's constituency.

* * *

[1] "*FAQ*" in this section refers to posted prepared solutions to the most frequently-received inquiries from customers

[2] To ensure that future changes to the posted contact information are shared by them.

[3] Methods suggested include options to click on "contact us," and/or initiate web chat.

[4] Abbreviated "RSS" and refers to automated notifications of newly posted web page content provided to customers who opt to receive them

[5] Includes short web page loading times and minimal need for scrolling

[6] Including misspellings commonly used by customers

FUTURE THOUGHTS

Mobile applications, video, social media, and other relatively new channels for serving government's customers will be followed by still others, some not yet even envisioned. The continuing deluge of new contact methods makes it more essential than ever for us to discern and apply the voices of our evolving customers across *all* demographics and channels when considering the role of new innovations for interaction. In the words of the Committee, we must:

> "*… realize the challenges of the road ahead, recognize them as greater opportunities, and embrace the goal to continually seek and foster responsiveness to the needs and preferences of government's customers.*"

The Committee also identified our greatest resource for doing so:

> "*The talent and dedication of people at the front lines — both those who interact with the customer and those who administer customer self-service — are pivotal to the effectiveness of customer support accomplished there.*"

We must be vigilant to ensure that each "*next big shiny thing*" is not carelessly applied as a cost-saver — but instead thoughtfully as a multiplier of service effectiveness. Historically, government has often found that the ultimate cost of designing services *wrong* and then trying to fix them is far greater than if they had been designed *right* from the perspective of the customer at the outset. Surveys have shown, for instance, that the live human option is *needed* by constituents who are confused by automation and/or are dealing with a personal crisis.

Customers bring a common need when they touch us — *a quick, accurate, courteous solution.* The perennial ingredients for delivering this are t*eamwork, technical excellence, and customer focus.* The core tenet of *all* customer contact service is *people helping people.* The organization's *culture* is the ultimate determinant of success based upon the value it places on the satisfaction of the *people* at *both* ends of the contact channel.

In order to reach our collective full potential for future success, we must as a community recognize the following:

Our signature product is knowledge packaged in culture

To all of my friends and colleagues in government contact services, good luck and god speed as *we* press ahead to serve *all.*

APPENDIX ONE

FEDERAL DEPARTMENTS AND AGENCIES REPRESENTED ON THE COMMITTEE

Bureau of Labor Statistics

Census Bureau

Centers for Disease Control and Prevention

Centers for Medicare and Medicaid Services

Defense Finance and Accounting Service

Defense Information Systems Agency

Department of Agriculture

Department of Education

Department of Health and Human Services

Department of Housing and Urban Development

Department of Justice

Department of Labor

Department of Treasury

Economic and Statistics Administration

Energy Information Administration

Environmental Protection Agency

Federal Trade Commission

Food and Drug Administration

General Services Administration

Government Printing Office

Internal Revenue Service

International Trade Administration

National Archives

National Institutes of Health

National Library of Medicine

National Oceanic and Atmospheric Administration

Office of Personnel Management

Office of Thrift Supervision

Railroad Retirement Board

Small Business Administration

Smithsonian Institution (a trust establishment)

Social Security Administration

U. S. Geological Survey

U. S. Postal Service

Veterans Benefits Administration

APPENDIX TWO

REASONABLE EFFORT

[Reproduced in part from the original Committee report]

As managers of Government customer support, the members of the Committee were challenged to assume the perspective of the customer in determining what "should be" at Government's front lines. Although we deal intrinsically with the special fiduciary responsibilities to balance cost efficiency with effectiveness, which are unique to the public sector, the word "resource" arose frequently in Committee deliberations on a wide range of practices and approaches. Given that Government funds customer support (with very few exceptions) with public funds, some key standards, guidelines, and recommendations, which we have endorsed, specify what we believe represents a *"best try" within reasonable expense* to respond to needs and expectations of customers.

The Committee does not want our endorsed practices and approaches to customer support to become "unfunded mandates." They should instead be applied as a tool for serving customers with available resources in the spirit of one of our key standards:

Customer Support Resource Optimization

Application of limited resources across customer contact channels should be optimized based upon agency size, mission, and customer feedback. Topics and volume of customer inquiries should be tracked for use in forecasting contact volumes and scheduling customer support resources to handle them.

The enticement to resource and utilize our endorsed practices and approaches will, we hope, lie ultimately in the impressiveness of the results from doing so.

APPENDIX THREE

LINES OF BUSINESS IN GOVERNMENT CONTACT SERVICES

This list is adapted from pioneering work by my good friend Robert Smudde, to whom I am most grateful for sharing it.

1. **Information**
Transfer of information between government and customer.

2. **Benefits**
Payments and/or services that accrue to customers.

3. **Duty**
Interactions which are required of customers.

4. **Commercial**
Specific services or items for which customers directly pay government.

5. **Intergovernmental**

Interactions among government, law enforcement, and/or military organizations.

6. **Emergency**

Response to destruction or imminent threat to life and/or property.

7. **Other**

Interactions not included in any of the other six types above.

APPENDIX FOUR

LEVEL OF ENDORSEMENT FOR EACH SERVICE PROVISION

The three levels of endorsement cited below were defined by the Committee as follows, in descending order of emphasis:

<u>Standard</u>:   "*S*"   All organizations should adhere

<u>Guideline</u>:   "*G*"   Demonstrated positive impact on customer satisfaction

<u>Recommendation</u>:   "*R*"   Suggested improvement at organizational discretion

Section One – All Contact Services

Measures

1. S

2. S

Service Quality

1. S	6. S	11. S
2. R	7. S	12. G
3. R	8. S	13. R
4. G	9. S	
5. S	10. G	

Customer Complaints

1. S	4. S	7. G
2. G	5. S	8. G
3. S	6. G	

Internal Processes

1. R	3. S	5. S
2. S	4. S	

Resource Allocation

1. S

2. S

3. G

Written Communications

1. S   4. S   7. G

2. R   5. S

3. S   6. S

Language Services

1. G

2. G

3. R

Section Two – Telephone Services

Measures

1. G   4. S

2. G   5. S

3. R

Telephone Accessibility

1. S

2. S

3. R

Call Transfers

S

Recorded Messages

1. G   4. S

2. S

3. S

IVRS

1. S   4. R

2. R

3. S

VOIP

1. S

2. S

Section Three – Email and Web Response Form Services

Measures

1. S

2. S

Email

1. G   4. R   7. S

2. S   5. S   8. R

3. S   6. S   9. R

              10. R

Web Response Forms

1. G   3. G   6. S

2. S   4. S   7. G

        5. G   8. G

Section Four – Mail and Facsimile Services

Measures

1. S

2. S

Other Provisions

1. S

2. S

3. S

Section Five – Walk-In Services

Measures

1. G

2. G

Other Provisions

1. S   4. G   7. G

2. G   5. G   8. S

3. R   6. G

Section Six – Web Services

Measures

1. S

2. S

Posted Contact Information

1. S   4. S

2. S

3. S

FAQs

1. S   4. S   7. G

2. R   5. G   8. R

3. S   6. G   9. R

RSS

1. S   4. R

2. S

3. S

Web Chat

1. S   4. R

2. S

3. S

Web Site Utility

1. S

2. G

3. R

ABOUT THE AUTHOR

Daryl Covey grew up in Tulsa, Oklahoma. During his early years, he enjoyed fishing, visiting his grandfather's farm, and camping with the Boy Scouts – all of which instilled a special appreciation for the elements. After a tornado passed within a block of his home, he became interested in a career as one of the voices of the Weather Bureau issuing "tornado alerts" on the *radio* — which, in that era, was every kid's almost-constant companion.

After graduating from high school, Daryl completed a degree in meteorology and was hired by the National Weather Service (successor of the Weather Bureau). Within a few weeks after graduation, he began a thirty eight year career working in six states successively as a weather forecaster, air traffic control meteorologist, training manager, and ultimately founding manager of one of the most highly recognized help desks in government. Along the way he issued tornado warnings live on the radio!

Assuming the help desk position opened a whole new direction in Daryl's life. When he was tasked to establish it in the late 1980s, the only other visible help desks (at least in government) supported information technology, which was just fully emerging onto the world scene. Resources on effective customer support were few, benchmarking and sharing of practices were sparse, and information technology was only a part of the complex new system he was charged to support. Thus began a personal quest of over twenty years — which continues today — to learn and help improve how government cares for customers. It has led to interactions with organizations at all levels of government, partnerships with many entities focused on customer contact services, and the founding of a global community of practice devoted to the sharing of effective practices among the people who serve governments' customers.

Daryl holds a graduate degree from the University of Wisconsin and is a graduate of the Federal Executive Institute. He is retired from government but continues to speak and serve on behalf of government customer contact services wherever he can help to make a difference. When he's not doing that, you'll find him on the family farm in central Oklahoma, chairing the local fire protection and rural water district boards, or fishing Lake Tenkiller.

ACRONYMS

CzRM
Citizen Relationship Management

FAQ
Frequently-asked-questions

IVRS
Interactive Voice Response System

RSS
Really Simple Syndication

SGR
Standards, Guidelines, and Recommendations

VOIP
Voice-over-internet-protocol

GLOSSARY

Abandonment

A telephone customer in queue disconnects before reaching a live person

Automated Email Acknowledgement

Computer message advising sender that an email has been received by the organization

Automated Response

Computer message sent to user of automated customer interaction systems acknowledging the interaction and/or containing a prepared response appropriate to the inquiry

Business Days

Days during which all customer contact channels are available to customers

Business Hours

Hours during business days during which all customer contact channels are available to customers

Channel

Contact method by which a customer can interact with the organization

Citizen Relationship Management

The customer relationship management philosophy of creative and proactive customer service applied within the fiduciary and privacy constraints unique to government

Consensus

Unanimous agreement

Constituency

Segment of the population which is eligible to receive services of the organization

Contact Services

Capabilities for interaction offered to the constituency by the organization

"Contact Us"

A web page indicating all ways a customer can interact with the organization

Customer Facing Functionality

Structure and choices available to people contacting the organization via automated systems

Customer Relationship Management
Proactive approach to serving customers based on capture and processing of information about their preferences and prior interactions

Customer Service Representative
A person who interacts with customers on behalf of the organization

Event-based Surveys
Inquiries to obtain from a customer their level of satisfaction and/or other perspectives on a specific interaction with the organization

First Contact
The initial exchange of information between organization and customer regarding a specific customer issue

Frequently-asked-questions
Prepared solutions to the most frequently received inquiries from customers

Greeter
Person assigned to acknowledge the arrival of walk-in customers

Guideline

Middle level of endorsement which signifies a service provision which has been demonstrated to have positive impact on customer satisfaction

Home Page

The primary site of an organization's presence on the world-wide-web

Interactive Voice Response System

Automation for processing customer contacts in the telephone channel which offers customers service and/or information options among which they can select

Issue

A customer problem or inquiry

Lines of Business

Groups of organizations within government which are similar in function

Live Help

The option offered to a customer interacting with an automated system to instead interact with a person in real time

Loading Time
Speed at which content of a web page becomes fully visible to the customer after they select it

Navigation
The service pathway within an automated system which results from exercise of options selected by a customer in a given sequence

Plain Language
Communication at a level of complexity which is readily understandable by a majority of the constituency

Quality Assurance
Monitoring and/or measuring to ensure that services to customers meet or exceed standards of the organization

Queue
Customers who have connected with the organization's telephone channel and are awaiting service at a given time

Really Simple Syndication
Automated notifications of newly-posted web content provided to customers who opt to receive them

Recommendation
Lowest level of endorsement which signifies a service provision to be considered at the discretion of the organization

Resources
People, technology, and other organizational assets used in customer contact services

Return Call
Telephone contact with a customer made in response to a prior contact by that customer

Scrolling
Moving the cursor vertically on a web page

Self-Service
Customer interaction in which the customer can select prepared knowledge without direct human contact

Service Effectiveness
Success achieved in satisfying customers

Service Efficiency
Success achieved in optimizing use of organizational resources

Speech Recognition

Automated capability to apply words spoken by the customer to resolving their issue

Spikes

Sudden increases in customer contact volume which are not expected by the organization

Standard

Highest level of endorsement which signifies a service provision to which all organizations should adhere

Statutory

Prescribed by law

Style Guide

Organizational requirements for written interactions with customers

Toll-free Calling

The capability to contact the organization by telephone at no cost to the customer

Voice-over-internet-protocol

Transmission of speech across the internet

Web Chat
Capability to interact through the world-wide-web via text
entry exchanges which are visible to both parties in real time

Web Response Form
Entry point for structured text information provided by
customers interacting from the organization's web page for
later response

Web Self-Help
Structured knowledge posted on-line which is designed
to enable customers to resolve their issues without directly
contacting a person

REFERENCES

Call Center Management on Fast Forward
Brad Cleveland, ISBN 1-932558-06-3

Customer Surveying
Dr. Frederick C. Van Bennekom, ISBN 0-9713406-0-9

Governing by Network
Stephen Goldsmith and William D. Eggers, ISBN 0-8157-3128-0

Marketing in the Public Sector
Philip Kotler & Nancy Lee, ISBN 0-13-187515-9

Strategic Customer Service
John A. Goodman, ISBN 13: 978-0-8144-1333-3

The Best Service Is No Service
Bill Price & David Jaffe, ISBN 978-0-470-18908-5

The Science of Service
Wendi Pomerance Brick, ISBN 978-0-9831233-1-6

The Ultimate Customer Support Executive
Phil Verghis, ISBN 0-929306-34-1

Working Virtually
Trina Hoefling, ISBN 1-57922-032-0

THE CGOV COMMUNITY OF PRACTICE

Cgov was founded as a non-commercial outreach to foster networking and the sharing of effective practices among the people who provide customer contact services in government. It originated in the early 90's and today has a global base of participation spanning all government lines of business and all levels of government. Participation is free and open to everyone who serves government's customers.

You can learn more about *C*gov at www.cgovcop.org or by writing daryl@cgovcop.org.

"None of us is as smart as all of us."

—Ken Blanchard